D1266054

ANCIENT EGYPT

ANCIENT EGYPT

THE CRADLE OF CIVILIZATION

PETER MAVRIKIS

amber
BOOKS

Published by Amber Books Ltd
United House
North Road
London N7 9DP
United Kingdom
www.amberbooks.co.uk
Instagram: amberbooksltd
Facebook: amberbooks
Twitter: @amberbooks
Pinterest: amberbooksltd

Copyright © 2021 Amber Books Ltd.

All rights reserved. With the exception of quoting brief passages for the purpose of review,
no part of this publication may be reproduced without prior written permission from the
publisher. The information in this book is true and complete to the best of our knowledge.
All recommendations are made without any guarantee on the part of the author or publisher,
who also disclaim any liability incurred in connection with the use of this data or specific details.

ISBN: 978-1-83886-093-6

Project Editor: Michael Spilling
Designers: Gary Webb and Mark Batley
Picture Research: Terry Forshaw and Justin Willsdon

Printed in China

Contents

Introduction

The history, art and culture of ancient Egypt spanned thousands of years. Grand structures, including pyramids, temples and colossal statues have endured for thousands of years more, allowing people today to witness the achievements of this great ancient civilization. Some of the artifacts, temples and ruins detailed in this book will be easily recognizable – the Great Sphinx of Giza, the gold funerary mask of King Tutankhamun, and the walls covered by complex and colourful symbols and images known as hieroglyphs.

Many more visual examples dating from the Old Kingdom (2686–2181 BCE) to the end of the Greco-Roman Period (332 BCE–395 CE) may be less familiar, but will delight readers nonetheless.

The last 100 years has seen a flurry of discoveries. Some of these archaeological digs have spanned decades. Many are still ongoing. Thankfully, Egypt's hidden treasures are still being unearthed and will one day add to the catalogue of artifacts that Egyptologists will study and people will marvel at in the years to come.

ABOVE:
Hypostyle Hall, Temple of Hathor, Dendera

OPPOSITE:
**Colossal Statues of Rameses II,
Great Temple of Abu Simbel**

Old Kingdom

Many of the pyramids and monuments built thousands of years ago by the ancient Egyptians still stand and amaze the world. Nothing speaks more of the power of this ancient civilization than the time and effort – as well as the commitment to the science and art – required in building the Great Pyramids at Giza, the Great Sphinx, the multi-chambered *mastabas* (funerary structures), and solar ships. Many of these structures served as the transit sites of great rulers and their powerful civil servants before they embarked on their final journey to the afterlife.

It is because of the art and architectural wonders left behind by the Egyptians of the Old Kingdom (2686–2181 BCE) that we know so much about the ancient kings and their accomplishments, including Narmer, Seneferu, Djoser, Khufu, Khaefre, and the dozens others that ruled during the early dynasties. Powerful royal officers and loyal civil servants buried in *mastabas* left behind a record of their duties and achievements, and their life-size and detailed statues allow us to see what they looked like and how they dressed.

Though many ancient sites have been robbed through the ages, and the original building material may have been stolen, reappropriated or eroded with time, much from the Old Kingdom has survived, giving us a true glimpse of what life was like over 4,000 years ago during what can be considered a golden period of early human civilization.

OPPOSITE:
Pyramids, Giza Plateau
Built on a rocky elevated plain overlooking the Nile River, this vast funeral complex was used during the Fourth Dynasty (2613–2494 BCE) and is home to many of Egypt's most iconic ancient structures including the Great Pyramids, the Great Sphinx and the Tomb of Queen Khentkaus I.

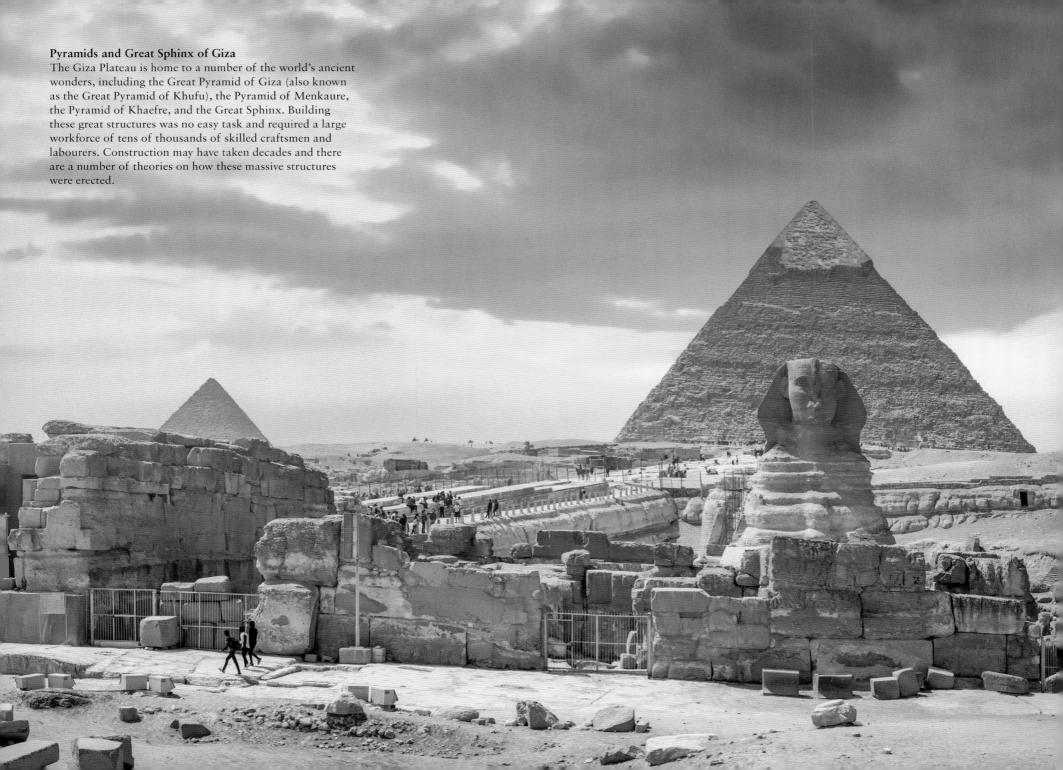

Pyramids and Great Sphinx of Giza
The Giza Plateau is home to a number of the world's ancient wonders, including the Great Pyramid of Giza (also known as the Great Pyramid of Khufu), the Pyramid of Menkaure, the Pyramid of Khaefre, and the Great Sphinx. Building these great structures was no easy task and required a large workforce of tens of thousands of skilled craftsmen and labourers. Construction may have taken decades and there are a number of theories on how these massive structures were erected.

RIGHT:
**Grand Gallery,
Great Pyramid of Khufu,
Giza Plateau**
Robbers and adventurers
bore their way into the
great pyramid long before
archaeologists began to
explore the inner chambers.
Although the pyramid
did not reveal any secret
treasures or the remains
of a buried pharaoh, it did
highlight the sophisticated
construction achieved
during the Old Kingdom.
Thick slabs of granite line
the slanted corridor and
rise up to a height of 8.8m
(29ft). The corridor is 2.1m
(7ft) wide and stretches
46.6m (153ft) long. The
Grand Gallery connects to
two other passages – one
leading to the 'Queen's
Chamber' and the other to
the 'King's Chamber'.

ABOVE:

Great Pyramid of Khufu, Giza Plateau

Built for the Egyptian pharaoh Khufu in 2567 BCE, this monument is the last surviving 'ancient wonder' of the world. It once stood at a height of 146.6m (481ft) with a square base of 230m (754.5ft). Though now about half a metre short of its original height, the pyramid consists of 2.3 million limestone blocks. After thousands of years of wind, sun and sand erosion, most of the blocks have lost their polished coating, which at one time gave the pyramid a brilliant white finish.

Queens' Pyramids, Giza Plateau

Located near the Great
Pyramid of Khufu,
these three pyramids are
significantly smaller in
size than the three great
pyramids, with the tallest
originally standing at a
height of 30m (98ft).
The northernmost pyramid
is attributed to Queen
Hetepheres, the mother of
King Khufu. The second
pyramid belongs to Queen
Meritites, the half-sister
and wife of Khufu. The
third pyramid is ascribed to
Queen Hanutsen, believed
to be the mother of Khaefre.
Inside each pyramid are
corridors lined in limestone
that lead to burial chambers.

Khufu Ship, Giza Pyramid Complex
This ritual solar ship built to ferry Khufu to the afterlife was discovered in 1954 at the base of the Great Pyramid of Giza (Khufu) and was sealed in a pit carved from bedrock. The find consisted of 1224 dismantled pieces of wood that were still intact after being buried for almost 4500 years. Dating back to around 2500 BCE, the ship is believed to belong to the great pharaoh Khufu. It took a restorer from the Egyptian Department of Antiquities almost 14 years to put the pieces together and reconstruct the funeral ship. Once rebuilt, the ship measured 44m (144ft) in length and 6m (19.5ft) in width.

LEFT:
Sheikh el-Balad, Saqqara Necropolis
Referred to as Sheikh el-Balad ('chief of the village') by the workmen that unearthed this discovery in the Saqqara Necropolis, the wooden statue depicts Ka-Aper, a chief lector priest in charge of reciting burial prayers. The statue is made out of sycamore wood. The eyes are made of opaque quartz and rock crystal, with the rims of the eyes inlaid with copper. This realistic figure dates back to the Fifth Dynasty.

Mastaba of Seshemnefer IV, Giza Plateau
Located at the foot of the Great Pyramid of Khufu, this burial site dates back to the Sixth Dynasty (2340 BCE) and serves as the final resting place for Seshemnefer IV, a highly ranked and favoured official who attended the pharaoh. Outside, separated by two columns, are two statues depicting Seshemnefer IV. Inside, visitors can view reliefs displaying scenes of his life, including hunting, harvesting and the slaughtering of bulls.

Light Show, Pyramids of Giza
Tourists from around the world can learn about the Pyramids of Giza – and also be entertained – by watching a light show narrated by an Egyptologist. In this image, laser lights project a pharaoh's head on to the Great Sphinx.

RIGHT:
Pyramid of Khaefre, Giza Plateau
Built for the great pharaoh Khaefre (r. 2555–2532 BCE) – the second son of Khufu and fourth king to rule during the Fourth Dynasty – this pyramid is the second largest in size after the Great Pyramid of Khufu. Dating back to around 2500 BCE, it has the distinction of appearing to be larger than the Great Pyramid of Khufu because it was constructed on a higher elevation on the Giza Plateau, giving it the appearance of having an extra 10m (33ft) in height. In actuality, the pyramid is 143m (471ft) tall.

ABOVE:

Pyramid of Menkaure, Giza Plateau
Completed in the twenty-sixth century BCE, this is the
smallest of the three great pyramids located on the Giza
Plateau. The Pyramid of Menkaure has a height of 65m
(213ft) and was built for King Menkaure, the son of
Khaefre and grandson of Khufu.

Khaefre Enthroned

This funerary statue of King Khaefre was made out of diorite, an extremely strong, dark-coloured igneous rock, believed to have been mined from quarries located hundreds of miles away from the Giza Plateau. The statue is life-size and stands 1.7m (5.5ft) tall. It depicts Khaefre sitting on his throne and wearing a royal headdress. The statue depicts Khaefre in the prime of life with a powerful physique matching this ruler's status as a god-king.

LEFT:

Triad of Menkaure

Made of schist, a hard metamorphic rock, this statue stands at a height of a little over 1m (3ft) and depicts King Menkaure with the goddess Hathor to the right and a female representation of the seventeenth *nome* (territorial division) of Upper Egypt to the left. Menkaure wears the white crown of Upper Egypt and is displayed as a fit and powerful ruler. Hathor wears a headdress of cow horns and a sun disk, while the female figure displays a standard representative of her *nome*.

Pyramid of Djedefre, Abu Rawash
Archaeologists believe that the Pyramid of Djedefre at one time matched the height of the Pyramid of Menkaure. Built during the Fourth Dynasty for the son of Khaefre, this once great pyramid now consists mostly of ruins and is a shadow of its former glory.

Unfinished Pyramids, Abusir
This ancient ruin is located near the Pyramid of Sahure and the Solar Temple of Userkaf. The unfinished pyramid is attributed to Shepseskare, who may have been the last pharaoh of the Fourth Dynasty or an early pharaoh of the Fifth Dynasty. The reign of Shepseskare is believed to have been short (one to seven years), resulting in the incomplete construction of the pyramid.

Pyramid of Neferirkare Kakai, Abusir

Built during the Fifth Dynasty for King Neferirkare ('Beautiful is the Soul of Re') Kakai, the pyramid is the tallest structure in Abusir. The pyramid originally stood at a height of 70m (230ft) with a base length of 105m (350ft). What remains today stands at a greatly reduced height of 50m (164ft). The unfinished structure was intended to be a step pyramid consisting of six layers. Beside it are two smaller pyramids built for Khentkaus and Neferefe.

OPPOSITE:

Pyramid of Djoser, Saqqara
Built in the twenty-seventh century BCE, this step pyramid consists of four sides and six tiers. Designed by Imhotep, the structure originally stood at a height of 62.5m (205ft). Today it stands as the tallest structure in the funerary complex.

RIGHT:

Mastaba of Rahotep, Rahotep and his Wife Nofret
This perfectly preserved statue was first unearthed in 1871. The husband, Rahotep, was a high official and bore the title 'son of the king', who at the time was Snofru. Though the title may have been honorific, he and his wife, Nofret, served the royal family and held several important positions.

OPPOSITE:

Tomb of Mereruka, Saqqara
A once powerful vizier who served King Teti (2345–2323 bce) during the Sixth Dynasty, Mereruka's tomb is the largest funerary site for someone that was not a member of the royal family. The mastaba contains 33 chambers, including this decorative room with a statue of the ancient Egyptian vizier.

LEFT:

Pyramid of Djoser, Saqqara
Also known as the Step Pyramid, this funerary site was originally intended to be a mastaba, but additional layers were added to the original roof to make the structure more visible from the capital city of Memphis.

ABOVE:

Wadjet Wall, Pyramid of Djoser, Saqqara

Wadjet, the cobra goddess of ancient Egypt, stands watch from the top of a wall, part of Djoser's funerary complex. The snake-headed deity was the patron goddess and protector of Lower Egypt and guardian of the pharaohs.

RIGHT:

Mortuary Temple, Pyramid of Djoser

Constructed during the Third Dynasty, the outer wall was built using stone instead of mud brick, which was the preferred building material at the time. The walls have a height of 10.5m (35ft) and the only entrance to the complex reveals a very narrow passage that opens to a walkway lined with a series of columns.

ABOVE:
Bent Pyramid, Dahshur
This structure has a unique design that differs from the smooth, straight-angled structures constructed during the Old Kingdom. Built for King Sneferu almost 4000 years ago, the lower part of the structure rises up to 47m (154ft) at an angle of 54 degrees, and has kept the smooth limestone found in other pyramids, while the rest of the structure slants at a 43-degree angle.

OPPOSITE:
Roofed Colonnade Entrance,
Djoser Pyramid Complex, Saqqara
Built by the architect Imhotep, the funerary complex of Djoser stretches 549m (1800ft) in length and 274m (900ft) in width. Massive column walls resembling reed bunches line the complex. There are 40 such columns in the structure, which are believed to represent the 40 *nomes* (territorial divisions) under King Djoser's rule.

Red Pyramid
Built by King Sneferu in 2590 BCE, this ancient monument is the third largest pyramid after the great pyramids of Khufu and Khaefre, and the largest pyramid in the Dahshur necropolis located 40km (25 miles) south of Cairo. Also called the North Pyramid, it is more commonly referred to as the Red Pyramid due to the red colour of the limestone that was used in its construction.

ALL PHOTOGRAPHS:

Saqqara Necropolis
This ancient necropolis from the Old Kingdom was built near the Nile River and served the city of Memphis. The complex contained numerous pyramids and a number of mastabas. Inside many of these funerary complexes are artifacts, including tombs that date back more than 4000 years. Most of the walls built into these ancient structures were also covered with carved artwork, including prayers and spells to aid the entombed as they travelled to the afterlife.

**Pyramid of Unas,
Saqqara Plateau**
This monument was built in
the twenty-fourth century
BCE by Pharaoh Unas, the last
king of the Fifth Dynasty.
Known to be the smallest
pyramid of the Old Kingdom,
the original structure stood
at a height of 43m (141ft).
The pyramid lies mostly in
ruins, either due to poor
construction or because much
of the material was reused for
other projects.

RIGHT:
**Sarcophagus of Unas,
Pyramid of Unas**
The black basalt sarcophagus was the final resting place for the ninth and final king of the Fifth Dynasty. When first discovered, archaeologists were amazed at the decorated walls and imagery found in the burial chamber.

OPPOSITE:
**Pyramid Hieroglyphics,
Pyramid of Unas**
This ancient burial chamber for King Unas displayed the earliest examples of what is referred to as Pyramid Text. In many cases, the religious text consisted of prayers and spells (283 'utterances') to protect the deceased king and help him travel to the afterlife.

Pyramid of Meidum
Also known as Sneferu's Pyramid, this structure was originally planned as a step pyramid but later changed to a true pyramid with smooth, symmetrical sides. The original structure has deteriorated but the monument still stands at a height of 65m (210ft). Sneferu was the first king of the Fourth Dynasty and the father of King Khufu.

RIGHT AND OPPOSITE TOP:

Cave of the Swimmers, Wadi Sura

About 600km (370 miles) west of the Nile River lies Wadi Sura ('Valley of the Pictures'). Here in the heart of Egypt's Western Desert is the Cave of Swimmers, a rock formation that includes numerous Neolithic cave drawings displaying people hunting, gathering and even swimming!

OPPOSITE BOTTOM:

Narmer Palette

Made around 3000 BCE, this carved artifact shows King Narmer wearing the White Crown of Upper Egypt and standing above a defeated enemy. Beside him is the god Horus, in the form of a falcon. On the other side, Narmer is seen wearing the Red Crown of Lower Egypt. possibly signifying the unification of Egypt during his rule. This carved artifact is 63.5cm (2ft) tall and is made of gray-green siltstone.

Middle Kingdom

Known as the 'time of unification', the Middle Kingdom brought peace and stability where Upper and Lower Egypt joined to form one kingdom ruled by the great pharaohs of the Eleventh and Twelfth dynasties (2125–1710 BCE). Pharaohs of the time include Mentuhotep I ('the Uniter of the Two Lands'), builder of the necropolis at Deir el-Bahari; and Senusret III, the warrior-king who built a strong army. Other great kings were Mentuhotep II, Amenemhat I, Senusret I, Intef and Amenemhat II.

Arts flourished during this golden age as sculptors chiselled massive rocks and developed the block statues now housed in museums around the world. Many of these solid, life-like figures survived for thousands of years, hidden under crumbling structures or buried beneath the desert sands. Temples, pyramids, obelisks, causeways and subterranean funerary chambers were built in massive complexes displaying the power and greatness of the kings of the Middle Kingdom, along with their loyal administrators and servants. It is during this time when stories of their lives, religious rituals, funerary rites, and visions of the afterlife were recorded and decorated the walls of temples and tombs alike. Today, we can see these lives illustrated in graphic form most famously on the walls of the Tomb of Khnumhotep II at Beni Hasan.

OPPOSITE:

Mortuary Temple of Mentuhotep II (Background), Deir el-Bahari

Known as the first ruler of the Eleventh Dynasty, Mentuhotep II chose to build the Deir el-Bahari complex beside the looming cliffs on the west bank of Thebes. The construction deviated from the use of pyramids: now the tomb was connected to the mortuary temple. In addition, the site included a causeway that led to the large courtyard that was once lined with sycamore trees.

Pyramid of Amenemhat III (Black Pyramid), Dahshur
The dark colour of the pyramid is due to the mud-brick and clay. Much like the pyramid of Amenemhat I, the structure did not prove to be as durable as the great pyramids of the Old Kingdom. Construction issues plagued the builders from the very beginning, including cracks and crumbling walls.

OPPOSITE:

Pectoral of Amenemhat III, Pyramid Complex, Dahshur
This intricate piece of neck jewellery was found in the tomb of Mereret, King Amenemhat's sister. It shows the goddess Nekhbet, depicted as a vulture, protectively spreading her wings over Amenemhat III as he strikes down his enemies.

RIGHT:

Pyramid of Amenemhat I, Lisht
Not much remains of the pyramid built for King Amenemhat I (1985–1955 BCE). Unlike earlier temples built from blocks of stone and encased in limestone, the material for this structure consists of mud-brick, which did not stand the test of time.

LEFT:
Osiride Pillar of Senusret I
The son of Amenemhat I, Senusret I was the second king of the Twelfth Dynasty (1956–1910 BCE). Records at the time indicate that Senusret was a peaceful king and ruled during a period of prosperity. This carved and painted image of Senusret is housed in the Luxor Museum.

OPPOSITE LEFT:
***Ka* Statue of Hor, Dahshur**
This wooden statue of King Hor dates back to the Thirteenth Dynasty (1795–1650 BCE) and displays the pharaoh's *ka* – vital force – as two upraised arms over each side of his head. The eyes of the statue are made of rock crystal and quartz.

OPPOSITE RIGHT:
Obelisk of Senusret I, Heliopolis
Located in Heliopolis – Greek for 'city of the sun' – this is the oldest standing obelisk in the world and is all that remains of this ancient religious centre. Erected almost 4000 years ago and made of red granite, this structure is 20.7m (68ft) tall. Weighing 120 tons, the monument stands in its original position, which is now inside a suburb of Cairo.

Pyramid of Senusret II
Located at the opening of the Hawar basin, near the modern town of Lahun, the builders of this pyramid took advantage of a natural limestone mound that was carved to form the four steps of the pyramid's base. Mud-brick, which has since eroded, was used for the upper half of the structure. Originally encased in white limestone, this outer layer was removed during the Nineteenth Dynasty and reused by Rameses II for other structures.

LEFT:

Tomb of Senusret III, Abydos

This 'hidden' tomb in Abydos dates back to 1850 BCE and is one of a kind due to its large size, measuring in at 200m (656ft) in length and 45m (145ft) in depth. First discovered in 1901, the tomb was not fully excavated until almost a century later. The interior walls are made of Tura limestone and Aswan quartzite. Massive 50-ton blocks of stone helped protect and conceal the tomb.

OPPOSITE:

Pectoral of Princess Mereret, Funerary Complex, Dahshur

Like the pectoral of Amenemhat III, this piece of neck jewellery was found hidden in the tomb of Mereret, and may have been a gift from her father King Senusret III. Two falcon-headed sphinxes subdue their enemies as the goddess Nekhbet, depicted as a vulture, hovers above carrying two *shens* – signs of protection – in her claws.

Beni Hasan Rock Tombs
Found on the east bank of the Nile River, this site is the location of 39 rock-cut tombs carved in the limestone cliffs for provincial governors and civil officials of the Eleventh and Twelfth dynasties of the Middle Kingdom. Many of these tombs have decorated walls depicting scenes of daily life, including hunting, recreation and war making.

**Hunting Wildfowl,
Tomb of Khnumhotep II,
Beni Hasan**
This vivid and colourful
scene from the tomb
of Khnumhotep II – a
chief magistrate of an
administrative *nome* – shows
imagery rich in a variety of
birds. There is a net attached
to the boat filled with the
caught waterfowl, displaying
the bounty set out for
Khnumhotep II in the afterlife.

ABOVE:

Tomb of Khnumhotep II, Beni Hasan

Khnumhotep II served as the chief administrator of the sixteenth *nome* of Upper Egypt during the reigns of Amenemhat II and Senusret II in the Twelfth Dynasty. Buried in a rock-cut tomb in Beni Hasan, the tomb walls are decorated with vivid scenes of Khnumhotep's life, as well as his burial ritual and imagery of the afterlife. This scene shows a part of a procession bringing offerings to the deceased.

The richly decorated walls found within the tomb highlight the great power that civil servants wielded under the authority of the kings from the Middle Kingdom. The walls of Khnumhotep II's tomb convey scenes of his life, including his family and relationship to the king, as well as imagery depicting the funeral rituals and passage to the afterlife.

OPPOSITE:

**Egyptian Soldiers,
Tomb of Mesehti, Asyut**

It was common for *nomarchs* – governors and chief magistrates – of the Middle Kingdom to recruit troops during times of unrest. These painted wooden sculptures were created to protect Mesehti, the *nomarch* of the thirteenth *nome* of Upper Egypt. Here, Egyptian spearmen holding hide shields stand guard in the tomb.

RIGHT:

**Forty Nubian Archers,
Tomb of Mesehti, Asyut**

In addition to the spear-carrying guards, Mesehti's tomb was also protected by 40 Nubian archers wearing red loincloths and carrying bows and arrows. The sculptors who carved these wooden figures used a variety of different facial expressions, creating a more realistic look.

OPPOSITE:

Stela of Abkau, Abydos
This intricately carved limestone slab dating back to the Eleventh Dynasty shows Abkau, the Overseer of Herds, with his wife Imemi, at a funerary meal. The couple is surrounded by family and servants that bring gifts for the afterlife. To the left, a woman is offering a necklace, while immediately facing Abkau, a servant is presenting the deceased with a cow's leg.

LEFT:

Model of Livestock Census, Tomb of Meketre, Deir el-Bahari
Meketre, a chief steward during the reign of Amenemhat I, watches while wood-carved figures of cattle with their herders march before him to be counted.

RIGHT:
**Colossal Statue of
Mentuhotep II,
Deir el-Bahari**
This colossal statue was
originally found in the
tomb of the king in Deir
el-Bahari. The life-size statue
is constructed of sandstone.
Seated on his throne, the
figure of Mentuhotep II is
painted in black and wears the
red crown of Lower Egypt.

OPPOSITE:
**Mortuary Temple
of Mentuhotep II,
Deir el-Bahari**
First discovered in the
mid-1800s with most of
the excavation taking place
in the early 1900s, this
terraced temple complex
was constructed for
Mentuhotep II during the
Eleventh Dynasty on a rocky
hillside near Deir el-Bahari.
The complex contains a
valley temple, a causeway,
a mortuary temple and an
underground burial chamber.

RIGHT AND OPPOSITE:

White Chapel of Senusret I, Karnak

Also referred to as the Jubilee Chapel, this structure was built during the Middle Kingdom but was demolished and used as filler material during the New Kingdom to build the third pylon (gate) of the Temple of Amun-Re. In 1927, the dismantled pieces were discovered in the temple, and by 1930 all the original pieces were removed and reassembled into the open-air museum now located at Karnak Temple. The limestone walls and columns display intricately carved hieroglyphics and art.

New Kingdom

Following a time of disunity during the Second Intermediate Period (1650–1550 BCE), the New Kingdom brought Egypt to the 'age of empire' as it greatly expanded its borders and reached deeper into Upper Egypt, Nubia and Asia. Thutmose III (r. 1479–1426 BCE) was a military ruler and conqueror who in 20 years launched 17 campaigns. His long reign lasted more than 50 years.

The New Kingdom marked a time of great architectural and cultural accomplishments, including building projects at Luxor, Abu Simbel, Abydos and Karnak, as well as the continued growth of funeral sites with their hidden tombs, massive sarcophagi, gold and silver treasure and walls covered in colourful and intricate images capturing the lives and the rituals of kings, queens, nobles, and those that served them.

For generations Egypt was united and prosperous. Kings continued to build great monuments commemorating their achievements. Rameses II, Horemheb, Seti I, Hatshepsut and other great rulers from the Eighteenth, Nineteenth and Twentieth dynasties left their mark through massive structures, stone sculptures and carved and painted images etched in walls at places such as the Temple of Nefertari, the Ramesseum, Tomb of Tutankhamun and the Temple of Hatshepsut.

OPPOSITE:
Great Temple, Abu Simbel
Constructed by Rameses II (1279–1213 BCE) in the far south of Egypt in ancient Nubia, four colossal statues of the pharaoh guard the entrance of the Great Temple. Carved into the sandstone cliffs above the Nile River, each statue is 20m (65ft) high. In the 1960s, the site was in danger of being flooded when the Aswan High Dam was being built. International technical support helped save the temple by disassembling the structure and moving it to higher ground.

ALL PHOTOGRAPHS:

Pharaoh Rameses II, Memphis
Housed in a museum specifically built to protect it, this giant
statue of Rameses the Great was discovered in 1820 by Italian
explorer and Egyptologist Giovanni Battista Caviglia. Carved
out of limestone and measuring 10m (32.8ft) long, the statue
broke from its base and is displayed on its back.

LEFT:

Tomb of Horemheb, Saqqara Necropolis

Horemheb (r. 1319–1292 BCE) was the last king of the Eighteenth Dynasty and at one time served as commander of the army under Tutankhamen. His ascent to power came through marriage. Buried in the Saqqara Necropolis, his tomb is decorated with colourful paintings that have withstood the test of time. In this image, located in the northeast wall of the antechamber, Horemheb faces the goddess Hathor (left) while to the right, he makes an offering to the sky god Horus.

ABOVE:

Temple of Seti I, Abydos

Seti I (1290–1279 BCE) started the construction, which was completed during the rule of his son, Rameses II. Dedicated to Osiris, who was believed to be buried in Abydos, the temple is considered by many as the most impressive ancient structure still standing from the New Kingdom period. Massive columns line the inside of the temple and lead to chambers within the structure. Natural light also illuminates the interior of the structure, entering through holes cut in the ceiling. This engineering and architectural feat helps illustrate the ingenuity of the ancient builders.

ALL PHOTOGRAPHS:
Temple of Seti I, Abydos
Carved into the walls within the temple is the 'king's table' a list of 76 of the kings of ancient Egypt. Also known as the 'kings list', this record of rulers has helped scholars and archaeologists learn much about Egypt's past. Names on the list include Khufu, Sneferu, Amenhotep and Seti; however, this list is far from complete as it has omitted – perhaps purposely – a number of Egypt's most powerful and well-known rulers, including Tutankhamen, Akhenaten and Hatshepsut.

LEFT:

Statue of Thutmose III, Karnak

Known as a great military leader and the king who ruled over more territory than any other pharaoh, this stunning statue immortalizes Thutmose's youth and vitality. The statue was discovered in 1904 in the courtyard of the Karnak temple and is now on display at the Luxor Museum.

OPPOSITE FAR LEFT:

Obelisk of Hatshepsut, Karnak

Erected by female ruler Hatshepsut (1473–1458 BCE) and carved from pink granite quarried far away at Aswan, this ancient monument is 28.6m (93.8ft) tall and weighs 343 tons. It is located in the Big Temple of Amon.

OPPOSITE RIGHT:

Statue of Rameses II, Memphis

This giant statue of the great pharaoh Rameses II, carved 3200 years ago, was discovered in 1820 near Memphis, 20km (12 miles) south of Cairo. The statue is made of red granite, is 9m (30ft) tall, and weighs 83 tons. In 2018, the statue was moved to the Grand Egyptian Museum in Giza.

**Festival Hall
of Thutmose III, Karnak**
This ancient monument was
named by Thutmose III as 'the
most splendid of monuments'
and was built in honour
of the pharaoh and used
annually for the Opet Festival
honouring the Egyptian gods.
The structure was originally
surrounded by dozens of
square-shaped columns that
supported the massive roof
and rounded interior pillars
leading to chambers.

LEFT:

**Seventh Pylon,
Thutmose III, Karnak**
Thutmose III was a great
warrior-king of Egypt,
conquering lands beyond
Egypt's borders, including
Palestine and Syria. Here he
is shown wearing the red
crown and attacking his
enemies with a club.

OPPOSITE:

Temple of Khonsu, Karnak
Built by Rameses III, this
temple measures 18m (59ft)
in height and 34.5m (113ft)
in width. At one time, the
courtyard was bordered by
28 columns. To the right of
the entrance are the remains
of a row of sphinx statues.

RIGHT:
Chair of Princess Sitamun, Luxor
This elegant wooden chair belonged to Sitamun, the daughter of Amenhotep III, and was discovered in the tomb of her grandparents (mother's parents) Yuya and Tuya. The legs of the chair are carved in the shape of lions' paws. The backside of the chair shows a double image of Princess Sitamun receiving a gift from a servant.

RIGHT:
Colossi of Memnon, Luxor
For centuries, these giant stone statues were attributed to the mythical Greek hero Memnon, though in actuality they embody the image of Amenhotep III. Rising 18m (59ft) from the ground, these statues were part of a larger temple complex that was destroyed by an earthquake in 29 BCE. Though both statues were significantly damaged by the event, they have managed to survive the test of time.

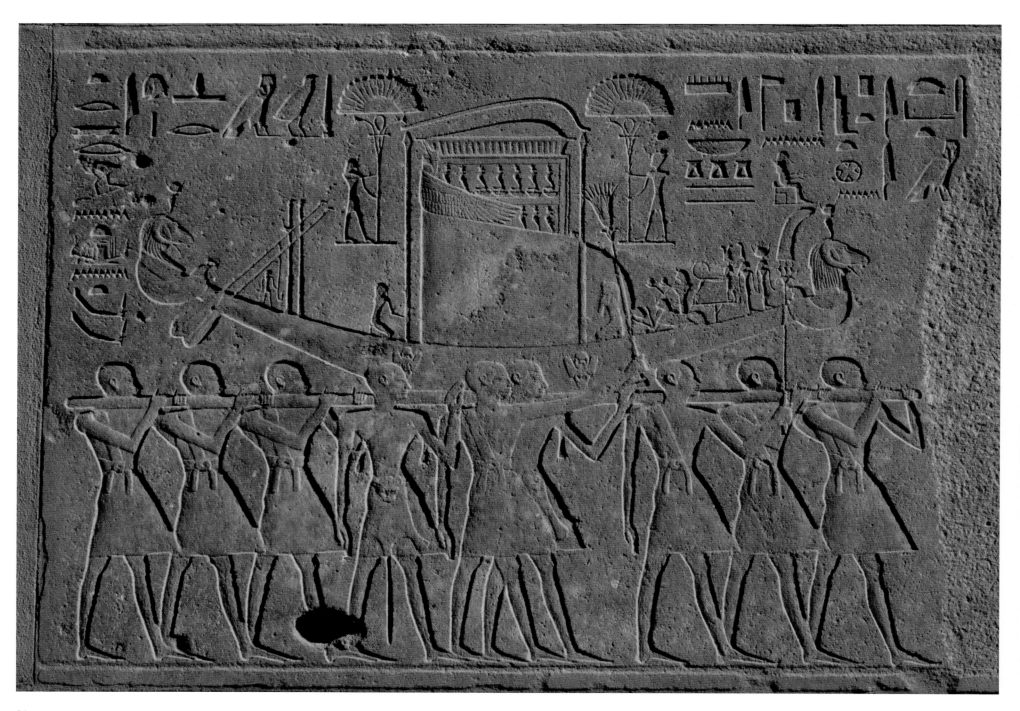

OPPOSITE:

Red Chapel of Hatshepsut, Karnak

Constructed during the reign of the fifth pharaoh of the Eighteenth Dynasty, the rock-cut chapel is covered with reliefs that display the events and accomplishments of the female-pharoah's life. The walls also show religious rituals, including this detailed carving of servants carrying the sacred boat of the god Amun-Re through the streets of Thebes during a religious festival.

RIGHT:

Statue of Amenhotep IV

Unlike earlier kings that worshipped the pantheon of Egyptian deities, Amenhotep IV (1352–1336 BCE) – also known as Akhenaten 'Servant of Aten' – is believed to have favoured the monotheistic worship of the sun god Aten. In addition to being the king, he also declared that Aten only speaks through Akhenaten, thus eliminating the priesthood and making himself a god-king. In this image, Amenhotep IV is presented as youthful, fit and even happy.

**Solar Court,
Luxor Temple**
This open-air structure
follows a peristyle design
with rows of papyrus
columns lined on three sides
of the court. The Solar Court
measures 52 x 46m (170 x
151ft) and has a total of 60
columns. Built around 1400
BCE, this outdoor museum
is one of the most visited
historical sites in Egypt.

Great Hypostyle Hall, Karnak

Massive decorated and intricately carved columns made of sandstone still remain standing in what is believed to be one of the largest religious sites of the ancient world. Built during the reign of Seti I, but completed by his son Rameses II, the complex is dominated by 134 columns in the form of papyrus stalks. Dozens of giant columns standing 20m (70ft) line the inside of the hall. Each immense column is richly detailed from its base to the ceiling. Though at one time brightly painted, the images of kings, queens, deities and their stories and rituals are still clearly visible.

Luxor Temple
The building of this grand temple was initiated by Amenhotep III but was continued by several other pharaohs, including Tutankhamen and Rameses II. In the front of the temple are two giant statues of Rameses II positioned between – and behind – two obelisks, though only one remains standing at the temple.

Constructed during the Eighteenth Dynasty, this statue (*left*) is one of the two seated figures of Rameses II standing watch on each side of the temple entrance. Carved from pink granite, this portrayal of the ancient pharaoh is 14m (46ft) tall and depicts the ruler wearing the traditional royal headdress.

Temple of Merenptah
Built for the thirteenth son of Rameses II, and successor to
the throne, Merenptah (reigned 1213–1203 BCE) was the fourth
pharaoh of the Nineteenth Dynasty and ruled for ten years.
Unfortunately, not much remains of the ancient structures.
All of the buildings in this site have been destroyed as a result
of flooding caused by the Nile River.

Victory Stele of Merenptah, Thebes
Discovered in 1896, this ancient artifact provides a record of Pharaoh Merenptah's military campaigns and victories against the Libyan tribesmen. Also known as the 'Israel Stele', many scholars believe that the twenty-seventh line includes a hieroglyphic inscription of Israel.

Tomb of Thutmose III, Theban Necropolis
Discovered by French Egyptologist Victor Loret in 1897, the ancient tomb of Thutmose III was ransacked by robbers thousands of years ago. What was left were discarded wooden statues, broken pottery and destroyed models. The main item left in the tomb was the empty sarcophagus. Made of quartzite, the tomb is painted red and covered in intricately carved hieroglyphics.

OPPPOSITE:

**Interior, Temple
of Hatshepsut,
Deir el-Bahari**
This painted relief shows
Egyptian soldiers on an
expedition to the Land of
Punt. Unfortunately, many
images of Hatshepsut that
were part of these reliefs were
destroyed by her successor
Thutmose III.

LEFT:

**Hathor Chapel,
Temple of Thutmose III,
Deir el-Bahari**
Located on the southern
side of the second level, the
chapel is dedicated to the cow
goddess Hathor, also known
as the deity of love, beauty
and music. Built during the
reign of Thutmose III (1479–
1426 BCE), the wall art in this
image shows the pharaoh
presenting the goddess with
an offering.

ALL PHOTOGRAPHS:

Mortuary Temple of Hatshepsut, Deir el-Bahari
Built for the Eighteenth Dynasty pharaoh Hatshepsut
(died 1458 BCE), the funerary complex took 15 years to complete.
The building consists of three levels reaching a height of 29.5m
(97ft). At one time the first level on the ground floor would have been
surrounded by well-kept trees and shrubbery. A causeway running
roughly 30m (100ft) connects the different tiers of the structure.

Deir el-Medina
Located on the West Bank of the Nile River near Thebes, this ancient village housed the artisans, labourers and craftsmen that worked on the royal tombs in the Valley of the Kings, along with their families. This well-preserved ancient village offers a glimpse of what life was like for the ordinary Egyptians living during the period of the New Kingdom.

PREVIOUS PAGES:
Tomb of Ramose, Theban Necropolis
Ramose was a governor and vizier that served under the rule of Amenhotep III and Amenhotep IV (Akhenaten) during the Eighteenth Dynasty. This image, found on the south wall of the nobleman's burial chamber, shows a funerary procession, including gifts for the afterlife being carried to the tomb. Above the procession, a golden coffin is dragged on a sled by servants.

RIGHT:
Tomb of Menma, Theban Necropolis
Built over 3000 years ago for an ancient Egyptian official named Menma, this ancient tomb is rich in imagery and vibrant with colour. The abundant display of art around the burial chamber helps depict scenes of Menma's life, family and duties, as well as imagery displaying burial rituals, the funerary procession, fishing and hunting, and the weighing of the heart.

RIGHT:

Funerary Mask of Tuya, Theban Necropolis

Tuya was a noblewoman and the mother of Tiya, the wife of Amenhotep III. Although she was not married to a king, Tuya and her husband Yuya were both held in high esteem by the pharaoh and buried in the Valley of the Kings.

Tomb of Tutankhamun, Valley of the Kings
British Egyptologist Howard Carter had spent a number of years excavating in the Valley of the Kings before he discovered the tomb of Tutankhamun (r. 1334–1325 BCE) in 1922. The find was a treasure trove of undisturbed ancient artifacts and riches. The sarcophagus held three coffins, with the central coffin made of solid gold and decorated with semiprecious stones, including turquois and lapis lazuli. Across his chest are two symbols of nobility and power – the crook and flail.

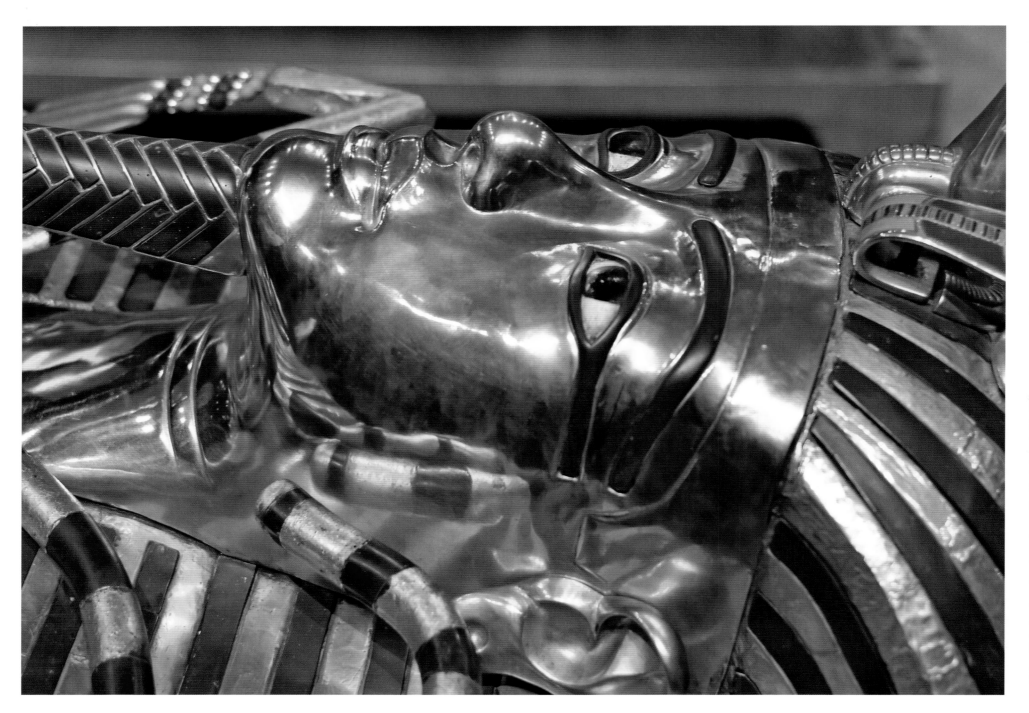

ALL PHOTOGRAPHS:

Golden Mask, Tomb of Tutankhamun, Valley of the Kings

The golden mask of the young king is one of the most recognizable treasures of Ancient Egypt. Made for Tutankhamun – son of Amenhotep IV and last ruler of his line – the golden mask was discovered in 1922 by British Egyptologist Howard Carter. Also referred to as a death mask, it weighs 10.23kg (22.5lbs) and portrays the ruler wearing the royal *neme* headdress and false beard.

On his forehead are depictions of the goddesses Nekbhet (vulture) and Wadjet (cobra). The back of the mask is covered with inscriptions from the *Book of the Dead*.

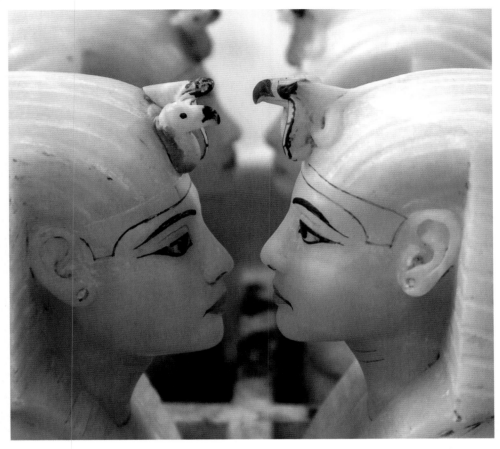

ALL PHOTOGRAPHS:
Tomb of Tutankhamun
OPPOSITE: Eight wooden fans were found in Tutankhamun's tomb. This wooden fan covered in gold shows the young king hunting ostriches while riding a chariot.

ABOVE: Made mostly from calcite (Egyptian alabaster) these canopic jars were used to store the internal organs – liver, stomach, lungs, intestines – of the ruler's body during the ritual mummification process.

RIGHT: This detail from the rear of the Golden Throne shows Tutankhamun sitting on his throne and attended by his wife, Ankhesenamun. The throne is made from wood but covered in gold and precious stones.

OPPOSITE:

**Ramesseum,
Theban Necropolis**
Rameses II serves as ruler of
Ancient Egypt for 67 years.
During his time as pharaoh,
he ordered the construction
of numerous structures,
including temples, monuments
and these massive, intricately
carved columns that still
maintain the weight of what
remains of the sandstone roof.

LEFT:

**Arcade, Ramesseum,
Theban Necropolis**
Located in Upper Egypt,
across from the Nile River and
near the city of Luxor, this site
served as the funerary temple
for Rameses II (r. 1279–1213
BCE), also known as Rameses
the Great. Today, most of the
site stands in ruin.

123

LEFT:

**Rameses II Statue,
Ramesseum,
Theban Necropolis**
Located in the Ramesseum
– the funerary temple of
Rameses II – all that remains
of the giant 17.5m (57ft)
seated statue are fragments
of the torso and feet. The
original statue is believed to
have weighed over 1000 tons.

OPPOSITE:

**Osirian Statues,
Temple of Hatshepsut,
Deir el-Bahari**
Built for Queen Hatshepsut
by her royal architect,
Senenmut, a series of statues
representing the image of the
god Osiris stand on the third
level of the temple. Here,
Osiris, god of fertility and
resurrection, is shown with
the crook and flail crossed
over his chest, both symbols
of power in ancient Egypt.

LEFT:

Statue of Meritamun, Ramesseum
Also called 'The White Princess' this limestone statue depicts the daughter of King Rameses II and Queen Nefertari. After the death of her mother, she took on the title 'Great Royal Wife'.

RIGHT:

Tomb of Nefertari, Valley of the Queens
Nefertari was Rameses II's first wife and held many titles, including 'Lady of the Two Lands', 'King's Great Wife' and 'Sweet of Love'. Pharaoh Rameses II build a great tomb for his wife surrounded by walls covered in colourful images, including this one of the goddess Maat, deity of truth, justice and order.

OPPOSITE:
First Pylon (Detail), Medinet Habu
This relief carved on the first pylon of the Mortuary Temple of Rameses III shows the pharaoh riding a chariot and hunting bull. Other images on the pillar depict the ruler's conflict with the Libyans and Sea Peoples.

ABOVE:
Medinet Habu
This location is home to a number of temples dating back to the Eighteenth Dynasty, but the most notable structure is the Mortuary Temple of Rameses III (r. 1186–1156 BCE).

The temple covers an area of 210 x 300 metres (700 x 1000ft). The structure's well-preserved walls are covered with images of the pharaoh's military exploits, including the defeat of the Sea Peoples during his rule.

ABOVE AND OPPOSITE:

Tomb of Seti I, East Valley of the Kings
Discovered by Giovanni Belzoni in 1817, the tomb of Seti I is one
of the most richly decorated burial chambers of ancient Egypt.
Unfortunately, Belzoni unintentionally damaged the colour of
many of the wall paintings when he attempted to make copies
by placing wet sheets of paper over the reliefs.

OPPOSITE:

Side Chamber, Tomb of Seti I
Pillars in the six-pillared room were decorated with scenes
dominated by Osiris. The ceiling is painted with astronomical
constellations and decans. In addition to the damage caused by
Belzoni, subsequent explorers and archaeologists also damaged
the site by cutting away pieces of the wall.

ALL PHOTOGRAPHS:
Entrace of the Great Temple, Abu Simbel
Built during the reign of Rameses II in the Nineteenth Dynasty, this enormous complex consisting of two temples – the Great Temple and the Small Temple (Temple of Nefertari) – is located in southern Egypt near the border with Sudan. The entrance of the Great Temple is guarded by four giant statues of Rameses II wearing the double crown of Upper and Lower Egypt. These massive statues measure 20m (65ft) in height.

LEFT:

**Great Temple,
Abu Simbel**

Eight Osirian pillars line the interior of the temple – four on each side. These columns link Rameses II to Osiris, the god of fertility, the dead and the afterlife.

OPPOSITE:

**Syrian Prisoners,
Great Temple,
Abu Simbel**

Reliefs found in the temple's interior depict the battles waged by Rameses II against the Hittites (Syria) at the Battle of Kadesh (1275 BCE), including victories in neighbouring Libya and Nubia. This image shows prisoners of war from one of the pharaoh's successful Syrian campaigns.

LEFT:
Great Temple, Abu Simbel
A second pillared hall within the temple shows beautiful and intricate examples of the art of the Nineteenth Dynasty. Many of the images depict religious rites and ceremonies, including offerings made to the gods.

OPPOSITE:
Temple of Nefertari, Abu Simbel
The second temple in the complex – known as the Small Temple – was built for Queen Nefertari and dedicated to the goddess of femininity, Hathor. Carved into the mountainside, four statues guard the entrance of the temple, including one depicting the queen, which stands 10m (32ft) high.

ALL PHOTOGRAPHS:
Temple of Nefertari, Abu Simbel
Richly etched walls line the interior of the temple, displaying images of Nefertari in the company of gods and goddesses. The two columns displayed opposite show images of the goddess Hathor, consort of the sun god Ra. Ancient Greeks identified Hathor with the goddess Aphrodite.

Late Period

The Third Intermediate Period (1069–664 BCE) saw the once unified empire divided in two. The influence and power of the High Priests of Amun grew until they gained ultimate control of Thebes and the surrounding lands. Egyptian kings maintained power in the north and ruled from Tanis to the Nile Delta. This period was a time of disarray, with Libyan kings taking control and eventually subduing the High Priests of Amun – but unity did not last long and soon the region was divided into city states.

The Late Period (664–332 BCE) consisted of six pharaohs of the Twenty-Sixth Dynasty, beginning with Psamtik I. The sixth century BCE would mark the Twenty-Seventh Dynasty, which would result from Archaemenid Persian conquest, effectively making Egypt a domain of the larger Persian Empire until the arrival of Alexander the Great and Macedonian conquest in 332 BCE.

Although foreign forces took over the land, Egyptian culture and traditions still dominated society through religion, architecture and the arts. In ancient places such as Saqqara, Luxor and Medinet Habu, pharaohs and nobles continued to build monuments, depict deities in art and bury the mummified bodies of the dead following funerary traditions practised for centuries.

OPPOSITE:
City of Tanis, Nile Delta
Located in the northeastern part of the Nile Delta, Tanis was the capital of ancient Egypt for over 300 years, beginning in the eleventh century BCE. Before that it was the capital of the fourteenth *nome* (province) of Lower Egypt.

City of Tanis, Nile Delta
Fallen and broken columns, along with scattered statues and ruins, are all that remains of this ancient site that once served as a capital city during the Late Period. Discovered in 1939, archaeologists unearthed several tombs rich in gold, silver and other treasure.

J·85821

LEFT:
Tomb of Psusennes I, Tanis
One of the tombs excavated in Tanis in 1940 belonged to the third king of the Twenty-First Dynasty, Psusennes I (1045–997 BCE). Left undisturbed for thousands of years, this ancient grave yielded a treasure-trove of gold and silver items.

RIGHT:
Stature of Osiris, Tomb of Psamtik, Saqqara
Dating back to the sixth century BCE, this statue of Osiris – lord of the dead and rebirth – was found buried in a shaft near the tomb of Psamtik III, the last pharaoh of the Twenty-Sixth Dynasty.

OPPOSITE:

Sarcophagus of Psusennes I, Tanis

Hidden from scavengers and robbers, this intact tomb of Psusennes I was discovered at the ancient capital at Tanis in 1940. Buried in the sarcophagus were a number of gold and silver items, including the funerary mask of the entombed pharaoh.

RIGHT:

Statue of Isis, Tomb of Psamtik, Saqqara

Found along with the statue of Osiris (see page 145), this statue of Isis – consort of Osiris – shows her with the cow's horns, which were usually attributed to the goddess Hathor.

LEFT AND OPPOSITE:

**Funerary Mask
of Psusennes I, Tanis**
The funerary mask of
Psusennes I was made of
gold, lapis lazuli, with
black-and-white glass used
to accentuate the eyes and
eyebrows. The sarcophagus
was discovered intact and
consists of an inner silver
coffin inlaid in gold. Unlike
other funerary sites, the
remains of Psusennes were
undisturbed until the tomb's
discovery in 1940.

**Communal Tombs,
Al-Ghoreifa, Tuna al-Gabal**
These recent discoveries
unearthed in 2020 contain
several sarcophagi, funerary
relics, jewellery, model figures
and over a dozen mummified
bodies. The remains are a
collection of tombs dedicated
to the high priests at the
Al-Ghoreifa area in the Tuna
al-Gabal archaeological site.

OVERLEAF:

**Ushabtis, Al-Ghoreifa,
Tuna al-Gabal**
Thousands of funerary
figurines were found buried
in the communal tombs.
Common during the Late
Period, the artifacts are made
of blue and green faience.
Many of the figurines
display engravings identifying
the deceased.

151

OPPOSITE:

Offertory Table, Chapels of the Divine Adoratrice, Medinet Habu
This black granite offering table was found outside one of the four chapels at Medinet Habu that were dedicated to the 'God's Wives of Amun' during the Third Intermediate Period (1069–664 BCE).

RIGHT:

Sarcophagus of Wennefer, Memphis, Saqqara
Dating to the Thirtieth Dynasty, this sarcophagus made of hard stone features a depiction of Wennefer – the High Priest of Osiris – as a human-headed bird. Funerary spells from the *Book of the Dead* are carved around the coffin.

FAR LEFT:
Avenue of Sphinxes, Luxor
Hundreds of ancient sphinx statues line both sides of the 2.7km (1.7 mile) avenue that link the temples of Luxor and Karnak. The sphinxes depict the head of pharaoh Nectanebo I with the body of a lion.

LEFT:
Gate of Nectanebo I, Temple of Amun, Medinet Habu
King Nectanebo I (380–362 BCE) was one of the last native Egyptian rulers. During his reign he built a wall around the Temple of Amun-Re. All that remains standing today is the portal, which at one time stood at a height of 20m (66ft).

LEFT:
Avenue of Sphinxes, Luxor
A number of the stone sphinxes have ram heads instead of the traditional human heads.

RIGHT:
First Pylon, Temple of Amun-Re, Karnak
Built by Nectanebo I, the first pylon is located at the main entrance of the Temple of Amun-Re. Though partially deteriorated, the pylon once reached a height of 38m (124ft).

LEFT:

Tomb of Pabasa, Hatshepsut's Temple, Deir el-Bahari
Pabasa was a noble that served during the reign of King Psamtik I and held the title 'Chief Steward of the God's Wife Nitocris'. This image found in the tomb shows a funerary scene with Pabasa surrounded by mourners.

OPPOSITE:

Tomb of Montuemhat, Theban Necropolis
Montuemhat was an Egyptian official who served as mayor of Thebes during the reign of Psamtik I. His tomb – designated TT34 and located in El-Assasif – contained a number of statues depicting the official.

**Tomb of Pabasa,
Hatshepsut's Temple,
Deir el-Bahari**
Finely carved reliefs line the
walls of the tomb. Many
of the images show deities,
funerary rites, as well as
colourful symbols and
patterns that have survived
for thousands of years.

OPPOSITE:
Head of Shabataka
This statue made of granite depicts King Shabataka (Shebitku), the second pharaoh of the Twenty-Fifth Dynasty that was started by his father, the Kushite king, Piye. The sculpture is currently located at the International Museum of Nubia in Aswan.

RIGHT:
Head of Taharqa, Karnak
Carved from black granite, this finely polished sculpture depicts the pharaoh wearing a Nubian cap crown. At one time, it is believed that the roughly carved crown was overlaid in gold.

PREVIOUS PAGES AND OPPOSITE:
**Temple of Hibis,
Kharga Oasis**
Built by the Persian King,
Darius I, to honour the
Egyptian fertility god,
Amun, this is one of the best
preserved sites from the Late
Period. A row gate that opens
to a pavilion where all of the
temple's original columns
still stand.

RIGHT:
**Tomb of Baenentyu,
Bahariya Oasis**
The wall painting shows
Anubis, god of death and
the underworld, embalming
the deceased. Overhead the
goddess Nekhbet, depicted
as a vulture, carries two
shens – signs of protection –
in her claws.

Greco-Roman Period

Ptolemaic rule began in Egypt in 305 BCE, after the death of Alexander the Great and the break-up of his empire. It lasted for nearly 300 years. The first pharaoh of this period was Ptolemy I Soter (305–282 BCE), who was a Macedonian-Greek general in Alexander's army. The last of the line was Ptolemy XV Caesarion – the son of Cleopatra VII Philopator and Julius Caesar – whose reign ended in 30 BCE with the Roman takeover of Egypt following the Battle of Alexandria.

This period in Egyptian history brought together three ancient civilizations, and monuments and temples display a melding of traditional ancient Egyptian culture with Greek and Roman influence. This fusion is also on display in paintings, statues and wall reliefs, and even in religious practice. No longer under the 'divine' rule of the pharaohs that dominated Egypt for thousands of years, the Roman rulers left behind a number of structures, including defensive buildings such as fortresses and towers, as well as towns with villas, bathhouses and theatres. Unlike the pyramids, *mastabas* and necropolises of earlier periods that celebrated the passing and rebirth of kings and deities, these Roman structures display how people lived, worked and managed Egypt.

Still, many Egyptian traditions continued under Roman rule. Temples were built, monuments were erected, and carved reliefs displayed hieroglyphs and images of ancient gods now interacting with Ptolemaic rulers and Roman emperors. This mingling would continue until the fourth century CE, when the new religion of Christianity started to gain ground.

OPPOSITE:
Temple of Esna
Twenty-four columns carved from red sandstone line the hypostyle hall inside the temple. The relief art on the walls show Ptolemaic and Roman rulers dressed in the garb of the pharaohs. Many of the images show these foreign emperors presenting offerings to the god Khnum.

OPPOSITE:

Catacombs, Kom el-Shoqafa, Alexandria

Located in the city of Alexandria, this is the largest Roman funerary complex in ancient Egypt. Utilized between the second to the fourth century CE, this ancient burial chamber – regarded as the principal tomb – shows signs of Greek, Roman and Egyptian influences.

RIGHT:

Catacombs, Serapeum, Amoud Al Sawari

These subterranean burial halls are located beneath the temple of Serapeum in Alexandria. The temple was dedicated to Serapis, a Greco-Egyptian deity and protector of the city.

LEFT:

Kom el-Dikka, Alexandria
The ruins of this ancient
site were unearthed during
building construction in 1967.
Dating back to the rule of
Hadrian (117–138 CE), the
area was reserved for the
wealthy, with lovely villas,
bathhouses and a theatre
(*pictured*).

OVERLEAF:

**Roman Baths,
Kom el-Dikka**
In addition to housing well-
off families during the
Greco-Roman period, the
site also provided the wealthy
with access to a bathhouse.
Known at the time as 'Park
of Pan', it is believed to have
been destroyed by a fire in
the third century CE.

175

LEFT:
Wadi el-Natrun
Dating back to the fourth century CE, this is one of the oldest Christian sites in Egypt. At one time, it was home to hermits choosing to live in isolation or as part of a monastic community. Today, the ruined site is surrounded by four monasteries following the Coptic Christian faith and traditions.

RIGHT:
Villa of the Birds, Kom el-Dikka
Recently restored and repaired from fire damage dating back over 1500 years, this site is known for its beautiful mosaics. Part of Kom el-Dikka, it is considered one of the best-preserved Roman villas of the period.

RIGHT:

Fort Babylon, Nile Delta
Located in Cairo, the fort was built by the Persian conquerors in the sixth century BCE. Since then, it had served as a Roman fortification and was eventually used to support some of the oldest churches in Egypt, including El-Muallaqa – the Hanging Church – built in the seventh century CE.

OVERLEAF:

Hieroglyphs, Athribis
This close-up found at the Ptolemaic Temple of Athribis shows the sky god Horus in the form of a falcon.

ABOVE:

Temple of Athribis

Located near the modern city of Sohag, the temple was built
when the Ptolemaic kings ruled Egypt for a span of 300 years.
Detailed relief work lines what remains of the walls, displaying
a mix of Hellenistic and Egyptian styles.

OPPOSITE:

Pompey's Pillar, Alexandria

Standing in the ruins of the Serapeum, this Roman triumphal
column was erected during the reign of Diocletian (284–305 CE).
Today it stands at a height of 26.8m (88ft), but at one time, the
pillar supported a 7m-tall (23ft) statute of the Roman emperor
suited in armour.

LEFT:

Temple of Sobek-Re, Dionysias, Faiyum
This damaged relief shows the crocodile god, Sobek. During the Greco-Roman period, many continued to worship the fused form of Sobek with Horus. This combined deity was Sobek-Ra.

OPPOSITE:

Catacombs of Kom el-Shoqafa, Alexandria
This painted wall scene depicts the mummification and preparation of a body for the afterlife. Within the catacombs are numerous examples of Egyptian imagery drawn with Greek- and Roman-style influences.

LEFT:

Funerary Portrait, Faiyum

Examples like this painting depicting the head of the deceased can be found in tombs throughout the region from the Roman period.

RIGHT:

Roman Temple, Qasr Qarun, Faiyum

What little remains of the ancient temple of Dionysus can be found near the location of a garrison town. The site at one time housed a sizable community that worshipped the Greco-Roman god of fertility, wine and festivities.

Wine Cistern, Roman Farm, El Heiz Oasis
Located near the ruins of a Roman fortress, this winery once served the garrisoned soldiers and administrators of the region. The excavated room consists of a depression that would have been used to collect, clean and handle the grapes before processing them into wine.

191

**Roman Fort, Daydamus,
Eastern Desert**
Built around the third century
CE, this fortress once covered
a four-acre area and housed
a large Roman garrison
stationed to defend this
distant outpost of the
Roman Empire.

OPPOSITE:
**Roman Fortress,
Ain Umm Labakha,
Kharga Oasis**
Made of mud-brick, the
ancient Roman military
structure still shows evidence
of thick defensive walls
and towers that at one
time helped keep the local
settlements and trade routes
protected from attack.

RIGHT:
Temple of Hathor, Dendera
Constructed in the Late
Ptolemaic period during the
reign of Ptolemy XII and
Cleopatra VII, the temple
also shows Roman influences.
The well-preserved temple
contains dedications to
Ptolemaic and Roman rulers
as well as traditional images
displaying Egyptian religious
rites and rituals.

Roman Birth House, Dendera

The traditional birth house – or *mammisi* – was built to honour the birth of a god or goddess's child. This *mammisi* is dedicated to Harsomptus, the son of Hathor and Horus.

OVERLEAF:

Temple of Hathor, Dendera

The entrance shown here was built during the reigns of the Roman emperors Domitian (81–96 CE) and Trajan (98–117 CE). In total, the complex covers an area of 40,000sq m (430,000sq ft) and includes several other structures.

RIGHT:
**Wall Murals,
Temple of Hathor**
Dating from the Ptolemaic period, this wall inside the temple showcases an intricate and colourful display of the pantheon of Egyptian gods.

OVERLEAF:
Ceiling, Great Hypostyle Hall, Dendera
Once covered by a thousand-year-old layer of black soot, the ceiling has been carefully cleaned to reveal the detailed and elaborate drawings and hieroglyphs, including the journey to the afterlife, and a row of ancient deities symbolic of the heavens facing the right eye of Horus. The outer hypostyle dates to the reign of Emperor Tiberius (14–37 CE).

LEFT:

Artifacts, Temple of Hathor, Dendera
Countless well-preserved artifacts, including carved reliefs and painted images, cover the complex from base to ceiling.

RIGHT:

Dendera Light, Temple of Hathor
Egyptologists will explain that the image on this carved stone relief displays a lotus flower with a wavy snake carved in the centre; but other observers see a light bulb and filament, and possibly evidence that the ancient Egyptians had electricity thousands of years before its modern use.

PREVIOUS PAGES,
LEFT AND OVERLEAF:
Temple of Khnum, Esna
Called Letopolis by the
Greeks, the site dates back
to earlier kingdoms but was
completed during the time
of Roman rule. One of the
more recent constructions
was the temple, build over
1800 years ago.

The structure includes a
hall with 24 lotus columns,
with palm capitals and wall
inscriptions and art displaying
the ancient Egyptian deities
and a number of Ptolemaic
rulers. Some of these
hieroglyphics date from the
time of Emperor Decius
(r. 249–251 CE).

OPPOSITE:
Temple of Edfu
Dedicated to Horus, who the Greeks equated to Apollo, this is the second-largest temple in Egypt and considered one of the best preserved. Giant pylons at the entrance of the temple reach a height of 36m (118ft) and detailed reliefs on the walls display carved images of the deities.

LEFT:
Statue of Horus, Temple of Edfu
Construction of the temple started during the reign of Ptolemy III Euergetes (246–222 BCE). This granite statue of the falcon-god Horus stands guard at the entrance of the temple.

LEFT AND OVERLEAF:
Temple of Kom Ombo, Aswan
Constructed during the late Ptolemaic dynasty (180–47 BCE), this unique temple originally consisted of two temples in one. The divided structure had two separate entrances, two courtyards, two halls and two sanctuaries – one dedicated to Horus and the other to the crocodile god Sobek. Hundreds of mummified crocodiles have been discovered buried beneath the ruins.

The site has seen its fair share of destruction through the centuries, including natural erosion, earthquakes, floods and the reuse of building material. Thankfully archaeologists are still uncovering buried parts of the complex.

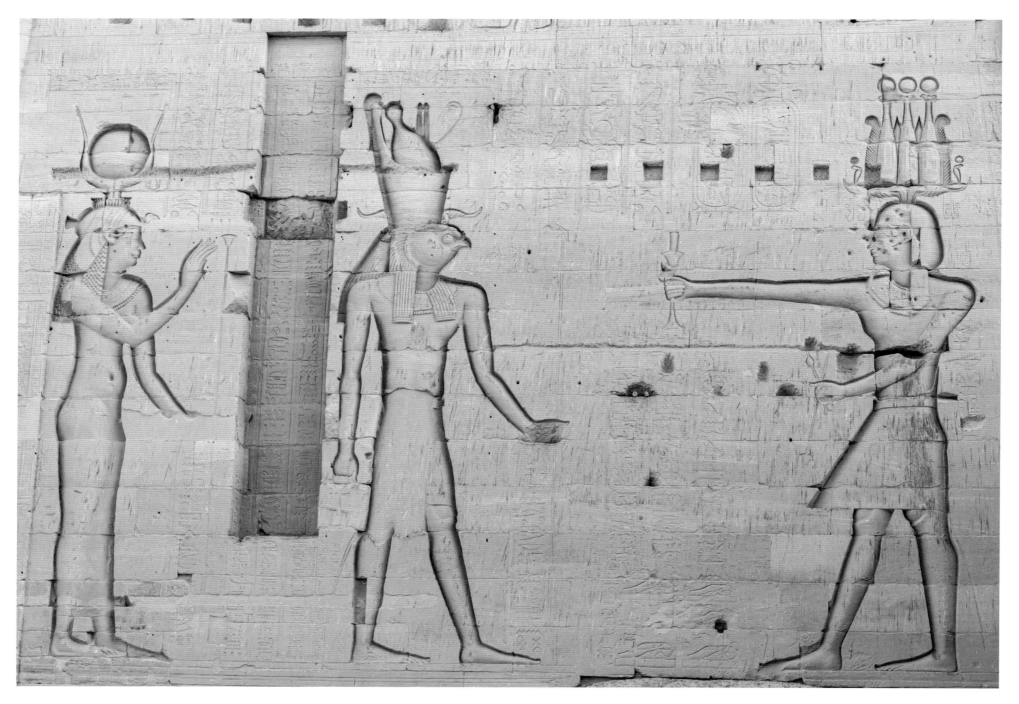

ALL PHOTOGRAPHS:
Temple of Philae, Aswan
The temple is believed to be one of the last built to follow classical Egyptian architectural style. Founded in the sixth century BCE to honour the goddess Isis, the temple was a sacred location for Egyptians, Romans and Nubians. Much of the surviving structures were built in the Ptolemaic era. No longer in its original location, the temple was moved to higher ground in the 1960s to avoid the destruction that would result from the Aswan High Dam project.

Temple of Kalabsha (Temple of Mandulis)
The temple was built around 30 BCE during the early Roman era. This relief carved on the wall of the temple shows the Nubian god, Mandulis (left), standing next to an offering table. On the other side is the depiction of an unidentified Nubian royal.

OPPOSITE:

Temple of Kalabsha

Considered a site to help heal the sick, Egyptians and Nubians would visit the temple and pray to Mandulis for a cure. Like many other ancient sites threatened by the Aswan High Dam, this temple was dismantled and moved to higher ground.

RIGHT:

Fortress of Kasr Ibrim, Lower Nubia

Originally a bustling cultural centre during the reign of King Taharqa (r. 690–664 BCE), the location was utilized by the Romans, who used the site's building material to create a fort. At one time the fort stood atop a cliff overlooking the Nile River, but due to flooding it is now just metres away from the water's edge.

Picture Credits

Alamy: 8 (Brian Lawrence), 12 (robertharding), 14/15 (travelpixs), 17 (robertharding), 26/27 (Mark Davidson), 30/31 (VPC photo), 33 (Jose Lucas), 37 (mrbeha/World History Archive), 39 & 42–43 (Paul Brown), 46 (Evren Kalinbacak), 50 (John Zada), 56 (Album), 58 (Heritage Image Partnership), 59 right (Alain Guilleux), 66 & 67 (ArtoKoloro),68/69 (Alain Guilleux), 70 & 73 (Heritage Image Partnership), 78 (Hackenberg-photo-cologne), 81 (W Michael Wiggins), 85 & 87 (Prisma Archivo), 90 (Angus McComiskey), 92 (Heritage Image Partnership), 103 (Alain Guilleux), 104/105 (Hemis),112/113 (Jean Dominique Dallet), 114 (Ivan Sebborn), 119 right (Jeff Fawcette), 120 (Imagedoc), 121 right (J Marshall-Tribaleye Images),122 (Angus McComiskey), 123 (imageBROKER), 131 (Ivan Sebborn), 132 (Hemis), 136 (Portis Imaging), 144 & 146 (Heritage Image Partnership), 148 (Ivan Sebborn), 149 (UPI), 160 & 161 (Magica), 164 (Stefano Ravera), 165 (Heritage Image Partnership), 174/175 (Linda Harms), 206/207 (Juergen Ritterbach), 210/211 (Prisma by Dukas Pressagentur), 222 (Art Directors & TRIP), 223 (Granger Historical Picture Archive)

Alamy/Agefotostock: 13, 59 left, 130, 140, 172, 187

Alamy/Mike P Shepherd: 51 top, 62, 64/65, 126, 142/143, 162/163, 168, 182/183, 192/193

Bridgeman Images: 107 (Sandro Vannini)

Creative Commons: 184 (Christian Leitz, Athribis Projekt)

Dreamstime: 18/19 & 22 (Anton Aleksenko), 24 (Christoph Lischetzi), 47 (Evren Kalinbacak), 48/49 (Prillfoto), 72 (Maria1986nyc), 74 (Christopher Bellette), 95 (Joe Sohm), 99 (Andrej Privizer), 100 (Christoph Lischetzhi), 115 (Mohamed Ahmed Soliman), 118 & 119 left (Neil Harrison), 121 left (Christophe Bellette), 138 & 139 (Emily Wilson),173 & 179 (Evgeniy Fesenko), 200/201 & 218 (EmilyWilson), 219 (Tomasz Czajkowki)

Getty: 57 (DEA/A.Dagli Orti), 63 (Barry Iverson), 71 (AFP), 76 (Werner Forman), 82 (Gavin Hellier/ robertharding), 88/89 (DEA/G Sioen), 127 (S Vannini), 145 (DEA/S.Vannini), 147 (DEA/A.Dagli Orti), 150–153 (Mohamed El-Shahed), 154 (DEA/C Sappa), 155 (Universallimages Group), 157 (De Agostini Picture Library), 169 (DEA.C.Sappa), 178 (Werner Forman),186 (DEA/C.Sappa), 188 (DEA/A.Dagli Orti), 189 (DEA/C.Sappa), 190/191 (DEA/S.Vannini)

iStock: 7 (Phooey), 52 (rchphoto), 86 left (cinoby), 125 (alan64), 135 (demerzel21), 213 (powerofforever)

Public Domain: 25, 51 bottom

Shutterstock: 6 (Cortyn), 10/11 (Alex Anton), 16 (TravelSH), 20/21 (Ihab Henri), 23 (Mirko Kuzmanovic), 28/29 (Iurii Kazakov), 32 (Danita Delmont), 34 (Sergey-73), 35 (Luciano Mortula-LGM), 36 (Eric Valenne geostory), 38 & 40/41 (Homo Cosmicas), 44/45 (Ryu K), 54/55 (Merlin74), 60/61 (Victor V. Hoguns Zhugin), 75 (Leonid Andronov), 77 (Iurii Kazakov), 80 (EvrenKalinbacak), 83 (achiaos), 84 (EvrenKalinbacak), 86 right (eugen-z), 91 (eFesenko), 93 (Zhukov Oleg), 94 (Vladimir Wrangel), 96/97 (Felix Lipov), 98 (noemosu), 101 (agsaz),102 (Diego Fiore), 106 (Vladimir Korostyshevskiy), 108 (agsaz), 109 (TomaszCzakowski), 110/111 (Vladimir Melnik), 116/117 (Nick Brundle), 124 (Bill McKelvie), 128 (GonzaloBuzonni), 129 (Witr), 133 (Anton_Ivanov), 134 (Lesleyanne Ryan),137 (Emily Marie Wilson), 156 (Joseph Sohm), 158 (PeskyMonkey), 159 (suronin), 166/167 (Anton_Ivanov), 170 (JasonHealy), 173, 176/177, 179 & 180/181 (eFesenko), 185 (kerenby), 194 (Cortyn), 195 (akimov Konstantin), 196/197 & 198/199 (Merlin74), 202/203 (Oksana Galiulina)), 204 (Olga Margulis), 205 (Abrilla), 208/209 (Stig Alenas), 212 (eugen-z), 214/215 (John Le), 216/217 (agsaz), 220–221 (Nestor Noci)